To Bill.
Thankyou for your e
I hope you find this *useful*

JOHN NEWTON

Evangelical Spirituality and Social Concern

by

Paul S. Taylor MA

THE WESLEY FELLOWSHIP

10A Barnet Road, Sheffield, Yorkshire S11 7RP

Occasional Paper No. 21

Wesley Fellowship Occasional Paper No. 21

Fig 1. *'On that day the Lord sent from on high and delivered me out of deep waters'* - John Newton's words recalling his perceived miraculous escape from drowning during an immense Atlantic storm that almost sank his ship *The Greyhound* on 10 March 1748 (Old Style), an anniversary he never let pass unnoticed for the rest of his life.

**John Newton: Evangelical Spirituality and Social Concern by Paul S. Taylor MA
Illustrated and prepared for publication by William T. Graham BA, MEd**

ISBN 978 0 86071 658 7

**Published by The Wesley Fellowship
10A Barnet Road, Sheffield S11 7RP**

In association with, and printed by

**MOORLEYS
Print & Publishing**

23 Park Road, Ilkeston, Derbyshire DE7 5DA, England
0115 932 0643 - info@moorleys.co.uk - www.moorleys.co.uk

Foreword

The Wesley Fellowship is very grateful to Mr Paul Taylor for making his most interesting essay on the spirituality and social concern of John Newton available for publication. As an 'Occasional Paper' it is unusual, although not unique, in that it has not been first delivered as a lecture at one of the meetings of the Fellowship. Some may wonder: What has John Newton to do with the Wesleys? The best answer might be to start to find out by reading Paul Taylor's paper! Perhaps there's even scope here for a PhD proposal! Anyway, the reader will find that the author handles any differences in theology between John Wesley and John Newton in a way that is sympathetic to both men. This is an approach that echoes the 'catholic spirit' of John Wesley and John Newton, with their evangelical understanding of the gospel, and their common determination to work with all those who honoured Christ and promoted his kingdom, even if they differed in some doctrinal matters. Although John Wesley was more than twenty years older than Newton, both knew one another well and met on numerous occasions during the second half of the eighteenth-century. Wesley even offered Newton the opportunity to join the 'Methodists' as one of his preachers! Regarding social concern, John Wesley and John Newton had much in common – not least their attitude to see the slave trade and slavery abolished, a point well brought out in Paul Taylor's account. If one wonders if Charles Wesley and John Newton knew one another, perhaps it is evidence enough to remember that Josiah Bull informs us in his biography of Newton (1868, p. 289), that Newton was present on 5 April 1788 at the funeral and burial of the Rev. Charles Wesley held at Marylebone church, London. Newton was there (despite being unwell himself at the time, and the day bitterly cold with snow falling), not simply due to the two men being acquainted, but specifically because, 'It was Mr. Wesley's wish, expressed before his death, that his friend Mr. Newton should be one of the eight clergymen who were to bear the pall.' Of course, John Wesley, Charles Wesley and John Newton were each - in their own somewhat idiosyncratic ways - evangelical clergymen of the Church of England until they died. With regard to John Newton, it is worth noting that D. Bruce Hindmarsh has stated (*Oxford Dictionary of National Biography*, OUP, 2004) that Newton in his later years 'continued to represent an affable, winsome evangelicalism within the Church of England, and his Calvinism became, if anything, more moderate as he grew older', and that Newton is reported as saying that he 'used Calvinism in his ministry like sugar in his tea: "I do not give it alone and whole; but mixed and diluted" '. This is typical of Newton's kindly humour and informal turn of phrase – a characteristic that Paul Taylor brings out in his informative account of the life of the former slave trader, who, as Jonathan Aitken aptly puts it in the title of his recent (2007) biography of Newton, passed in his long life 'from disgrace to amazing grace'.

Bill Graham
Manchester, September 2011

Acknowledgements

This short monograph was first prepared in 1996 as part of the requirements for a Master of Arts degree awarded by the Victoria University of Manchester following studies at Nazarene Theological College, Didsbury. The author acknowledges with gratitude the knowledge and patience of the Principal and staff of the College. The present publication owes much to the author's colleagues and friends who have assisted with its preparation. Particular thanks are due to: Philip Poncellet, IT consultant; Andrew Irvine, manager of the Bethel Evangelical Church Bookshop, Wigston; William T. Graham, Executive member of the Wesley Fellowship; and Peter Newberry and the staff at Moorleys Print and Publishing, Ilkeston. Particulars of the Wesley Fellowship are to be found on the back cover of this publication.

Paul Taylor, Shearsby, August 2011

Picture Credits

The front cover illustration is an adaptation of a photograph taken by William T. Graham of a small framed engraved portrait, labelled 'Revd. John Newton. Aged 83', on display in Olney Parish Church.

Fig 1. The illustration of a ship on the verso of the title page is adapted from a portion of a painting, *Indiamen in a Heavy Sea* by Charles Brooking, held at The National Maritime Museum, Greenwich.

Fig 2. Photograph of Olney Parish Church by William T. Graham, 1 September 2011.

Fig 3. From a National Archives image of St Mary's Woolnoth memorial to John Newton at < http://www.nationalarchives.gov.uk/pathways/blackhistory/journeys/virt ual_tour_html/london/city.htm > accessed on 14.09.2011.

Fig 4. Is based on a 1981 drawing by C. Reg Perkins, published in Jim Styles, *Let's Talk About Olney's Amazing Curate* (a booklet published c. 1983 in aid of Olney Parish Church Heating Fund, obtainable from The

Cowper and Newton Museum, Orchard Side, Market Place, Olney, Buckinghamshire, MK46 4AJ).

Fig 7. From a 2010 water colour & pen sketch of St. Mary Woolnoth by Thomas Corrie, at < http://www.afewthoughts.co.uk/sketches/index.php?type=place&sel=St+Mary+Woolnoth> on 12.09.11.

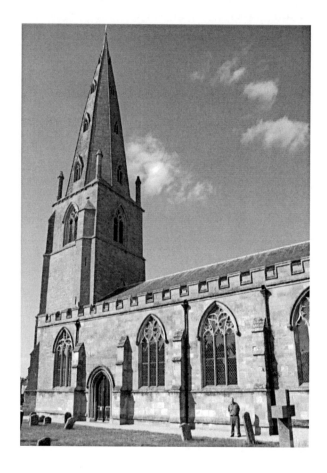

Fig 2. St Peter & St Paul Parish Church, Olney where John Newton was curate 1764-1779.
View taken in 2011 from near the present grave of Newton and his wife Mary

Contents

Foreword

Acknowledgements

Picture Credits

Preface

Part I   FORMATIVE INFLUENCES UP TO 1764

Part II   FOUNDATIONS OF SPIRITUALITY
  (i) Scripture
  (ii) Gospel

Part III   SOCIAL CONCERNS AND ACTION
  (i) Olney   (1764-1779)
  (ii) London   (1779-1807)

Postscript

Select Bibliography

Preface

This essay attempts to explore the evangelical spirituality of the Rev. John Newton (1725-1807), who as a young man was press-ganged into the Royal Navy, then deserted from the Royal Navy, became a slave himself, and later a slave-trader - then worked as a Government customs officer, finally becoming an Anglican clergyman, a noted hymn writer and slave abolitionist. In Part I the formative influences in Newton's early life are briefly outlined with comments. This is important because the biographical details and experiences were more than usually formative in his developing spirituality. His conversion in 1748 was a critical turning point and a transforming experience which permeated his subsequent life and ministry. In Part II the essay examines Newton's understanding of the importance of Scripture and the nature of the gospel which were the foundations on which he built his ministry in its varied aspects. Part III is an appraisal of Newton's spirituality as expressed in the concern he developed about the poverty of parishioners at Olney and the evil of the slave trade which he came to abhor and actively oppose, particularly in his later ministry at St Mary Woolnoth, in the City of London.

Part 1
FORMATIVE INFLUENCES UP TO 1764

John Newton was born in London on 24th July 1725 (O.S.[1]) and effectively converted to the Christian faith in 1748. Despite seven years of delays caused by unsympathetic bishops following his initial application to become a clergyman in the Church of England (and only then after decisive intervention with the archbishop of York on his behalf by the young evangelical nobleman Lord Dartmouth, prompted by Thomas Haweis), Newton received deacon's orders on 29 April 1764 from the bishop of Lincoln (in whose diocese lay the living and parish of Olney). Within two months (on 17 June 1764) Newton was made presbyter, and appointed curate-in-charge at Olney, Buckinghamshire. It was during this time at Olney that Newton befriended the poet William Cowper (who had been recently evangelically convicted but was in poor health). In 1767 the poet settled in Olney to be near Newton, and from 1771 the two men collaborated to compose a collection of hymns which were eventually published in 1779 as *Olney Hymns*. Soon after, on 8 December 1779, Newton was inducted into the benefice of St. Mary Woolnoth with St. Mary Woolchurch, in Lombard Street, London, where he became vicar and remained incumbent until his death in London on 21 December 1807.[2] He had married Mary

---

[1] In England the Gregorian calendar (New Style, 'N.S.') replaced the Julian (Old Style, 'O.S.') calendar in 1752. This caused an eleven-day change in the calendar - and some people even rioted because they thought they had lost eleven days of their life! However, when dealing with dates in John Newton's letters and diaries this difference needs to be remembered. For example, although the Atlantic storm which almost sank Newton's ship *The Greyhound* occurred on 10 March 1748 (O.S.), in later years (from 1752) he recorded the anniversary of the event as 21 March 1748, and 'never suffered it to pass wholly unnoticed' until he died. See: [John Newton]. *An Authentic Narrative*, Letter VIII, in: *Works*, ed. R. Cecil, Edinburgh, 1828, p. 18.

[2] Following the Great Fire of London in 1666, a committee under the chairmanship of Sir Christopher Wren was set up which chose just fifty-one churches, out of the 86 destroyed, to be rebuilt. St Mary Woolchurch Haw (which stood where the present Mansion House stands) was not one of those selected for rebuilding. Accordingly it was united with the nearby St Mary Woolnoth in Lombard Street, which was selected for repair – unfortunately, the patched-up structure proved unsafe and had to be demolished in 1711. The present building in Lombard Street (where from 1780-1807 John Newton was to become rector) was completely redesigned by Nicholas Hawksmoor in the English Baroque style, the work being completed in 1716.

Catlett of Chatham at St Margaret's Parish Church, Rochester, on 1 February 1750 (Old Style). Newton later wrote his own epitaph and requested that it be engraved on plain white marble and placed on a wall near the pulpit of his Lombard Street, London church, the combined benefice of St Mary Woolnoth with St Mary Woolchurch-Haw. It is still there to this day and reads:

JOHN NEWTON,
CLERK,
ONCE AN INFIDEL AND LIBERTINE,
A SERVANT OF SLAVES IN AFRICA,
WAS,
BY THE RICH MERCY OF OUR LORD AND SAVIOUR
JESUS CHRIST,
PRESERVED, RESTORED, PARDONED,
AND APPOINTED TO PREACH THE FAITH
HE HAD LONG LABOURED TO DESTROY.
HE MINISTERED
NEAR 16 YEARS AS CURATE AND VICAR
OF *OLNEY* IN *BUCKS*;
AND 28 YEARS AS RECTOR
OF THESE UNITED PARISHES.
ON FEB. THE FIRST 1750 HE MARRIED
MARY,
DAUGHTER OF THE LATE GEORGE CATLETT,
OF *CHATHAM, KENT.*
WHOM HE RESIGNED
TO THE LORD WHO GAVE HER,
ON DEC. THE 15TH 1790[3]

---

[3] See Fig. 3, which shows the memorial to John Newton still to be seen on a wall inside St Mary Woolnoth, Lombard Street, London. Note: John Newton was buried beside his wife, Mary Catlett, on 31 December 1807 in St Mary Woolnoth (she having died of cancer in 1790, after forty years of marriage); but on 25 January 1893, prompted by work extending the London underground railway under the church, both bodies were re-interred in the Buckinghamshire graveyard at Olney Parish Church at a spot marked by a large inscribed granite monument.

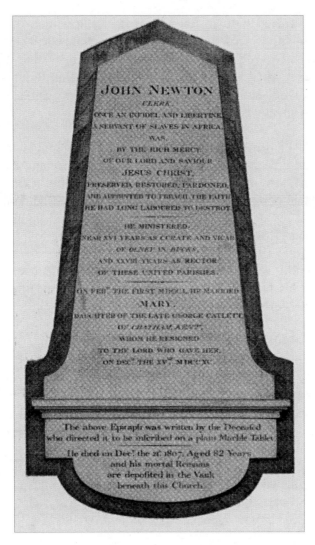

Fig 3. Memorial epitaph to John Newton at St Mary Woolnoth

John Newton's life of just over 82 years was contemporaneous with the 18th century revival under George Whitefield and John and Charles Wesley, and a return to evangelical religion in the Church of England under the influence of William Grimshaw, Thomas Haweis, William Romaine and others. Newton's mother, a Non-Conformist, died when he was seven years old - but not before she had taught him to read and pray and instructed him 'in the nurture and admonition of the Lord.' Thus were sown the seeds of Newton's future evangelical spirituality. If his mother was sensitive and pious, John Newton's father presented a vivid contrast and 'It is not easy to imagine how this Jesuit-trained sea captain, with his [acquired] haughty Spanish airs, came to marry a Dissenting woman who was obviously delicate.'[4]

Captain Newton was an aloof man who dealt severely with his only child. By the time John was born his father had become hardened by sea-faring life as master of ships engaged in the textile trade to Mediterranean ports. His Jesuit training had failed to cultivate any religious zeal but it had 'implanted a seed of personal dignity which in the grown man [had] blossomed into a slightly absurd stateliness' and sense of self-importance.[5] Captain Newton's second marriage was into an Essex family which did not readily accept his difficult son. Even so, John says of his father, 'he took great care of my morals but could not supply my mother's part.'[6]

At the age of thirteen John Newton went to sea with his father for the first time. Thus began a maritime career which was to last until 1755 when he was thirty years of age. During this eventful period Newton sailed on as many as seven different vessels, including trading ships and warships, and became embroiled in what was then the respectable business of slave-trading. His life was marked by a loss of early religious aspirations and what he describes as making a 'shipwreck of faith, hope and conscience.'[7] Yet he had periods of partial recovery especially in his youth. He records, '... I think, I took up and laid aside a religious profession three or four times before I was sixteen ... but all this while my heart was insincere.'[8]

It was when Newton was sixteen that he found himself attracted to Lord

---

[4] Bernard Martin, *John Newton: A Biography*, 1950, p. 5.

[5] Martin, *Newton*, 1950, p. 4.

[6] From: *An Authentic Narrative* [first published Aug. 1764], Letter II. See: *Works*, 1828, p. 4.

[7] From: *An Authentic Narrative*, Letter III. See: *Works*, 1828, p. 6.

[8] From: *An Authentic Narrative*, Letter II. See *Works*, 1828, p. 4.

Shaftesbury's *Characteristics*[9] and became a self-professed 'free thinker'. He only had to follow Shaftesbury's notions of 'freedom' and he would be happy. By that he meant free from his mother's pietistic training and from the guilt he felt at the sinfulness of his own life. Newton informs us that at that time 'this book was always in my hand', but his later evaluation of Shaftesbury's work, however, was quite different. He wrote, 'No immediate effect followed, but it operated like a slow poison and prepared the way for all that followed.'[10]

John Newton's life at sea, at first with his father, then press-ganged into the Navy, and later as mate and master of slave-trade vessels, coarsened his nature and shaped his depraved conduct. Despite the vulgarity of his companions, the rigours of the slave trade, the hazards of life at the mercy of the elements, and the influence of Shaftesbury, all was not lost. His desertion and the consequential humiliation of public flogging, his efforts to become more profane than his companions, the largely successful efforts to forget his mother's piety, all punctuated his maritime career; yet God would find him. This is how he later describes his predicament: 'I was miserable on all hands ... filled with the most excruciating passions, eager desire, bitter rage and black despair. Every hour exposed me to some new insult and hardship, with no hope of relief ... no friend to take my part ... I could perceive nothing but darkness and misery ... I was tempted to throw myself into the sea, which ... would put a period to all my sorrows at once. But the secret hand of God restrained me'.[11]

So one event heralded release and spiritual transformation, and another influence in his life kept him sane. This latter factor was that John Newton had 'fallen in love' with Mary Catlett when she was still a girl

---

[9] Anthony Ashley Cooper, 3rd Earl of Shaftesbury (1671–1713) was an English politician, philosopher and writer who in 1711 first published (anonymously, in three volumes) his *Characteristics of Men, Manners, Opinions, Times*. The *'Characteristics'* that John Newton appears to be referring to is probably the later edition that the earl's only son, the 4th Earl of Shaftesbury, republished in 1732. Note: the famous Christian philanthropist, the 7th Earl of Shaftesbury, was a descendant of these earlier nobles.

[10] From: *An Authentic Narrative*, Letter II. See: *Works*, 1828, p. 5.

[11] From: *Memoirs of the Rev. John Newton* by R. Cecil [first published 1808]. See: *Works*, 1828, p. 10.

of fourteen. She was a distant relative and Newton had been warmly welcomed into the Catlett home at Chatham because his mother and Mrs Catlett had been friends. His years at sea never dimmed his dream that one day he would marry Mary Catlett. Even though his wife-to-be only gave cautious approval to his advances, it was enough to keep his hopes of union with her alive, though not always enough to keep his chastity intact. The youthful and simple Mary was to become Newton's partner and support through all the ebbs and flows of life.

The Greyhound was a trading vessel which had been at sea for six months when Newton joined the ship on the African coast. The first twelve months aboard *The Greyhound* were spent in idleness, with little to read apart from a Bible and the classic text of *The Imitation of Christ* by Thomas à Kempis. So Newton devised new blasphemies to shock his crude companions. In 1748 *The Greyhound* set sail for England across the North Atlantic, but it was in hardly a sea worthy condition with its timbers shrunk by tropical suns. He discarded à Kempis because 'he could not bear the force of the inference' that there might be truth in these Christian ideas.[12] And so he turned again to Lord Shaftsbury's more comfortable *Characteristics*. During the night of 10th March 1748 (O.S.) a storm of unusual ferocity lashed against the frail ship. Newton and his companions battled to keep out the storm. He records, 'about nine o'clock, being almost spent with cold and labour I went to speak with the Captain ... I said, almost without meaning, "If this will not do, the Lord have mercy on us." This ... was the first desire I had breathed for mercy for the space of many years'. As Bernard Martin makes clear, this 'rudimentary prayer was crucial', and it marked the beginning of a profound change in Newton's life.[13] The ship, against all the odds, was saved and eventually limped into harbour in Lough Swilly, Co. Donegal.[14] The words of Jesus had struck Newton forcibly 'If ye, then, being evil know how to give good gifts unto your children; how much more shall your heavenly Father give the Holy Spirit to them that ask Him?' If this book is true, Newton thought, I must take God at

---

[12] Martin, *Newton*, 1950, 69.

[13] Martin, *Newton*, 1950, 71.

[14] *The Greyhound* needed six weeks of repairs before it could put to sea again, eventually reaching Liverpool at the end of May 1748. From: *Memoirs*. See: *Works*, 1828, p. 26.

his word and ask for the Holy Spirit. Some years later, Newton wrote:

> I stood in need of a mighty Saviour and such a one I found in the
> New Testament ... I was no longer an infidel ... I heartily
> renounced my former profaneness ... I was sorry for my past
> misspent life, and purposed an immediate reformation ... I was
> affected by a sense of my more enormous sins; but I was little
> aware of the innate evils of my heart ... I cannot consider myself
> to have been a believer, in the full sense of the word, till a
> considerable time afterwards.[15]

John Newton returned to sea as Mate, and eventually ship's Master, of
The Brownlow. Despite his new resolves he fell away yet again, until a
fever bringing him near to death 'broke the fatal charm and once more
brought me to myself.' From that time he says, 'I have been delivered
from the power and domination of sin .... It was the powerful grace of
God which preserved me from any further black declensions.'[16]

Newton's mother had desired that her only son should be called into the
ministry of the Church. After his sea-faring days were over, and during
the period from 1755 when he was Tide Surveyor in Liverpool, John
Newton slowly discovered a desire to serve God in the ministry. George
Whitefield and John Wesley in turn were invited by Newton to preach
in Liverpool. He was drawn to both evangelists, to Whitefield in
particular, and (with reservations) to Wesley. Newton also at the time
became associated with independent churches in Yorkshire and
Warwick before eventually, years later, being ordained by the Bishop of
Lincoln into the curacy at Olney. At the time of his ordination in 1764,
John Newton was almost forty years of age and had been married for
fourteen years.

---

[15] Newton's words are cited in: Martin, *Newton*, 1950, 79.
[16] Newton's words are cited in: Martin, *Newton*, 1950, pp.87-8.

Part 2
FOUNDATIONS OF SPIRITUALITY

(i) Scripture

In the introduction to his celebrated *Sermons on Several Occasions* (1746), John Wesley described himself as '*homo unius libri*' (a man of one book[17]), though he read far more widely than most of his contemporaries. The same paradox applies to John Newton, but perhaps not with the same sharp tension - because Wesley had all the advantages as a pupil at the famous Charterhouse School, followed by his time at the University of Oxford as student and don, whereas Newton's formal education had ended by the time he was ten. As a Tide Surveyor at Liverpool from 1755-1764, Newton's staple spiritual diet was scripture. Newton also set himself at this time to study Greek, Hebrew and Latin, and devoted his life to the 'prosecution of spiritual knowledge'. This devotion, he writes, 'divorced me from the classics and mathematics'. Newton's aim was to obtain 'the signification [i.e. significance] of scriptural words and phrases.' In both Greek and Hebrew he became reasonably proficient; sufficient he says to 'judge for myself the meaning of any passage ...' However, he confirms that during this period, between his times on duty as a Tide Surveyor at Liverpool, 'I have accustomed myself chiefly to writing, and have not found time to read many books besides the scriptures.'[18]

During 1759 Newton prepared a series of six sermons which he had not been able to actually preach, explaining that, 'the views I then had are now over-ruled.' And so, in 1760, he published them in print form instead as *Discourses, & c., as intended for the pulpit* - although he explains that if he had anticipated this, 'I should have chosen to put my sentences in another form', adding that the subjects chosen were important in that 'what they contain is agreeable to scripture, reason and

---

[17] See: [John Wesley], *The Works of John Wesley*, Sermons I, ed. Albert C. Outler, 1984, p. 105.

[18] From: *An Authentic Narrative*, Letter XIV. See: *Works*, 1828, p. 32.

experience'.[19] It is of interest to compare this 'Trinitarian' formula with the unofficial Wesleyan quadrilateral (which included 'tradition'), and the Lambeth formula of scripture, creeds, sacraments and episcopacy. Whatever Newton was, he was not a man who paid undue attention to ecclesiastical traditions! Some insights into Newton's attitude to Scripture can be found in Sermon 5 and Sermon 6 in this collection, which are both based on John 5:39 and entitled 'On Searching the Scriptures'.[20] The Bible formed a sure foundation for a developing spirituality and aligned Newton with orthodox evangelism.

Newton clearly points out in these sermons that Scripture must be approached with 'Sincerity', meaning 'a real desire to be instructed' and to 'submit' to what is read. Further (citing Prov. 2; Psalm 111; and 2 Tim. 3), he states that Scripture must be searched with 'Diligence'. Newton uses a mining analogy of digging and examining; he advocates assiduous reading (digging) and awakened meditation (examining). The hermeneutic was to take notice of the circumstances, occasions and application of what is read. 'Meditation' involved receiving the doctrines, submitting to the reproofs and obeying the precepts of Scripture. All examination which falls short of this may educate the mind but will be of little use: citing Grotius[21], Newton exclaims: 'Alas! I have worked all my life in much labour to no purpose'. Newton also stipulates 'Humility' because Scripture is a revelation of God, and 'If God leaves us to ourselves, we are all ignorance and darkness'. Newton affirms that the study of Scripture was for the purpose of knowing ourselves, including our sinfulness and ignorance. He advocates prayer as an important means of discerning the Word of God. For Newton's spirituality, prayer was as indispensable for the understanding of Scripture as for the whole of life. In this series of six sermons, Newton gives a key to the unlocking of Scripture, stating that: 'Christ is the main purpose and subject of both Scripture as a whole and each particular book.' He adds that, in the Old Testament, Christ is to be

---

[19] From: Preface to *Discourses , &c., or Sermons, as intended for the Pulpit.* See: *Works*, 1828, p. 312.

[20] From: *Discourses, &c., or Sermons, as intended for the Pulpit*, Sermon V, and Sermon VI. See: *Works*, 1828, pp. 333-43.

[21] Dutch scholar Hugo Grotius (1583–1645) was, during the seventeenth century and later, a towering figure in philosophy, political theory, law and associated fields.

found in the prophetic, typological and ceremonials; and Newton believed that the New Testament shows all these fulfilled in Jesus of Nazareth.

To summarise: Newton writes, 'The sense of the sacred writings lies too deep for a captious, superficial, volatile survey; it must be a search, a scrutiny; a humble, diligent, sincere and persevering enquiry, or no satisfaction can be expected.'[22] Newton's Christology was objective in that he searched the Scriptures to find Christ there; but it was subjective too, because in a letter written early in 1764 (a few months before he was ordained and became curate at Olney) he was able to recall that in 1755, when he was first settled in a house in Liverpool and finding that his employment offered him some leisure time, he concluded that in spiritual terms he was 'still a learner', and had 'attained but very little', and so he adopted 'the apostle's determination, "to know nothing but Jesus Christ, and him crucified"', and henceforth to devoting his life 'to the prosecution of spiritual knowledge' and resolving 'to pursue nothing but in subservience to this main design.'[23]

(ii) Gospel

Newton's understanding of the Gospel, derived as it was from Scripture and experience, had an Augustinian focus on sin and grace. Entering into and maintaining salvation from sin, by God's grace in Christ, formed the essential substance of Newton's ministry of preaching, correspondence, pastoring, hymnology and social action. John Newton found that much of his correspondence (which became a major part of his ministry), could be published because his letters were often returned to him (and he had no easy means in those times of copying!). Similarly, many of his sermons were prepared by him for publication. Furthermore, most of his hymns, with those of Cowper, composed at Olney, although primarily at least written for singing in the prayer meetings which became an important part of Olney church life under Newton's leadership, were eventually published in 1779 as the *Olney*

---

[22] From: *Discourses, &c., or Sermons, as intended for the Pulpit*, Sermon V. See: *Works*, 1828, p. 337.

[23] From: *An Authentic Narrative*, Letter XIV (dated February 2, 1764). See: *Works*, 1828, p. 32.

Hymns.[24] It is in these letters, sermons and hymns that his recurring themes of sin and grace are to be found. For Newton, the human personality could not be understood without recognising its sinfulness, and God could not be known - apart from the revelation He gave to fallen humanity of His grace in the death and resurrection of the Lord Jesus Christ.

Newton's Letters 33 and 34, published under the pseudonym 'Omicron'[25], describe how Newton understood man in his 'fallen state'. Fallen man is depraved by sin, and yet he is still 'capable of great things; his understanding, will, affections, imagination and memory are noble and amazing powers'.[26] When, however, man is considered in a 'moral light', accountable to God, he is a 'monster' and a 'fool'. In a particularly revealing passage, Newton explains that '...there is no fool like the sinner, who prefers the toys of earth to happiness of heaven: who is held in bondage by the foolish customs of the world, and is more afraid of the breath of man than of the wrath of God.'[27] Newton's somewhat colourful language is not yet exhausted; man in his fallen estate is a 'beast', and looks no higher than 'sensual gratification' and 'obstinacy'.[28] Fallen man, Newton says with daring vocabulary, '...resembles Satan in pride..., in malice... and... this diabolical disposition often proceeds to murder ... envy... and cruelty'.[29] This may seem to a modern mind a dark and pessimistic view of human sinfulness yet it comes out of Newton's own experiences; he had learned how his own heart was 'deceitful and desperately wicked'. Even so, Newton, it

---

[24] Newton in his Preface reminds his readers that 'the whole number were composed by two persons only...with the desire of promoting the faith and comfort of sincere Christians.' See: [John Newton], *Olney Hymns*, 1779, pp. v-vi. Remarkably, the *Olney Hymns* are *still* in print in 2011 (in facsimile form, and beautifully bound), and available more than 230 years after they were first published from The Cowper & Newton Museum, Olney, Buckinghamshire.

[25] From: *Forty-One Letters on Religious Subjects*. [First pub. London, 1807; some originally published by John Newton, under the Signatures of 'Omicron' (c.1774), and more under 'Vigil' (c.1785)]. Letter 33 and Letter 34, both under the title of 'Man in his fallen state'. See: *Works*, 1828, pp. 108-112.

[26] *Works*, 1828, p. 108.

[27] *Works*, 1828, p. 108.

[28] *Works*, 1828, pp. 108-9.

[29] *Works*, 1828, p. 109.

would appear, deliberately painted the colours at the dark end of the rainbow, in order to contrast the bright and hopeful end of the spectrum. He writes, 'We cannot at present conceive how much we owe to guardian care of divine providence, that any of us are preserved in peace and safety for a single day, in such a world as this.'[30] To be sure, Newton reassures us that it is not a hopeless condition, because: 'How wonderful is the love of God in giving His Son to die for such wretches! And how strong and absolute is the necessity of new birth if we would be happy!'[31] Can 'beasts' and 'devils' inherit the Kingdom of God? Newton assures his readers that they surely may because: 'Jesus is mighty to save. His grace can pardon the most aggravated offences....The gospel ...is still the power of God unto salvation...'.[32] And this is the heart of the gospel of grace gladly embraced by Newton and which vitally informs his spirituality. The transformation from a state of sinfulness to that of grace finds its expression in many of the Olney hymns. Here is an example from Newton:

> Our time in sin we wasted
> And fed upon the wind;
> Until his love we tasted,
> No comfort could we find;
> That now we stand to witness
> His power and grace to you;
> May you perceive its fitness?
> And call upon him too![33]

Such a verse could not stand comparison with the best of Isaac Watts or Charles Wesley, but its language is unambiguous and is not untypical of Newton, even when, in poetic terms, he is here somewhat below his own best.[34]

---

[30] *Works*, 1828, p. 109.

[31] *Works*, 1828, p. 110.

[32] *Works*, 1828, p. 112.

[33] From: *Olney Hymns in Three Books*, Book III, Hymn No. III, 'We Were Once as You Are.' Verse 4. See: *Works*, 1828, p. 605.

[34] Newton remarks that 'There is a style and manner suited to the composition of hymns, which may be more successfully, or at least more easily attained by a versifier, than by a poet. They should be hymns, not odes, if designed for public worship, and for use by plain people.' See: his Preface to *Olney Hymns*, 1779, p. vii.

It is, moreover, characteristic of the subjectivity and simplicity of much of Newton's work and is perhaps out of balance when compared with the apostolic insistence on a spirituality which is ecclesial as well as individual.

If sinfulness was dark and degrading, grace was bright and liberating. In Newton's thought the undeserved grace of God was pervasive. The idea of mercy was no less so. Grace and mercy were concomitants in the Gospel, two inseparable expressions of the love of God. If grace represented God's blessings on the undeserving, mercy was the withholding of punishment from the deserving. In Newton's spirituality, grace and mercy were bound up in the person and work of Christ.

Fig 4. The old vicarage at Olney in 1980; Rev. John Newton's home 1760-1779

OLNEY HYMNS,

I N

THREE BOOKS.

Book I. On felect Texts of Scripture.
Book II. On occafional Subjects.
Book III. On the Progrefs and Changes
of the Spiritual Life.

————————Cantabitis, Arcades, inquit,
Montibus hæc veftris : foli cantare periti
Arcades. O mihi tum quam molliter offa quiefcant,
Veftra meos olim fi fiftula dicat amores !
Virgil, Ecl. x. 31.

And they fang as it were a new fong before the
throne;—and no man could learn that fong,
but the redeemed from the earth. Rev. xiv. 3.

As forrowful—yet always rejoicing, 2 Cor. vi. 10.

L O N D O N :

Printed and Sold by W. Oliver, Nº 12, Bartholomew-Clofe ;
Sold alfo by J Buckland, Nº 57, Pater-nofter-Row ; and
J. Johnson, Nº 72, St Paul's Church-yard,

M DCC LXXIX.

Fig 5. Title Page of Newton & Cowper's *Olney Hymns*, 1779

14

In a sermon preached at Olney entitled *The Glory and Grace of God revealed in Jesus Christ* [35] Newton expounded his doctrine of grace, to him irresistible because it came from a sovereign God. In this, of course, he regarded Wesley as to be respected and honoured - but mistaken. Newton stands here in the line of Whitefield and moderate Calvinism. Newton teaches that the knowledge of God comes to sinful humanity in the person of Christ, and 'In Him the fullness of the Godhead dwells, and from Him, as light from the sun, the unsearchable riches of His goodness are communicated to indigent, unworthy sinners'; and 'The great God is pleased to manifest Himself in Christ as the God of grace.' Furthermore, this grace, Newton affirms, is many sided; it pardons, converts, restores and preserves; indeed God's grace 'finds the sinner in a helpless state, sitting in darkness and in the shadow of death'.[36] For Newton, grace pardons the guilt and subdues the power of sin, it binds up the 'broken heart' and restores the soul from wandering and makes the soul more than a conqueror over all opposition. In the end grace bestows the crown of everlasting life. Without the intervention of Christ in his life, death, resurrection and rule on behalf of sinners, grace could never have been known. Such is the transformation of spiritual life which Newton knew both from experience and from the Scripture. It is expressed nowhere more forcefully than in his most famous hymn. 'Amazing grace! ... That saved a wretch like me!'[37]

Grace and mercy, as Newton came to know them, though they were individually experienced, were to be communicated and shared, in the ecclesial settings of worship, prayer and preaching as well as in the daily contacts with parishioners in need. They were to be the motives of his daily caring ministry to the poor in his parish and the mainspring of his opposition to all forms of enslavement - whether as a result of personal foolishness or through an unjust society in which sinners became the inevitable victims of the sinfulness of others.

---

[35] From: *Sermons Preached in the Parish-Church of Olney, Buckinghamshire*, Sermon VIII. See: *Works*, 1828, p. 371.

[36] *Works*, 1828, p. 372.

[37] Newton's hymn, 'Amazing grace!' appears first in *Olney Hymns*, 1779, pp. 53-4, in Book I. On Select Passages of Scripture', under: ' I. Chronicles, Hymn XLI. Faith's review and expectation, Chap. xvii. 16, 17'.

Part 3
SOCIAL CONCERNS AND ACTIONS

(i) Olney (1764 - 1779)

Into John Newton's developing spirituality came an awareness that the work to which he had been appointed was to involve the task of standing with his parishioners in their poverty. Yet in Newton's spirituality lurked ambivalence to poverty. He could even write to a friend 'On the advantages of a state of poverty'[38], encouraging the reader to be content with 'sanctified poverty'. Poverty was honourable because it 'affords a peculiar advantage for glorifying God ... and is a comparatively safe state ... [because the poor] are able to live in more immediate dependence on God ... they have in general the greatest share in God's consolations ... ; though they have many trials and sufferings God has promised to make their strength equal to their day.' 'In a word,' he writes, 'you are not [really] poor but rich.'[39] On the other hand, the work of alleviating suffering was one in which he became engaged with characteristic zeal. In his Olney days Newton's concern was to provide the basic requirements for a reasonable standard of living for those who suffered deprivation. It was not until later that he discovered the need to deal with political policies which contributed to suffering.

In a letter of 1775, addressed to a Mrs P--- (and written with the serious rumblings of impending revolution in the British colonies in America in mind), John Newton writes, 'I meddle not with the disputes of party or concern myself with political maxims but such as are laid down in Scripture. There I read that righteousness exalteth a nation and that sin is a reproach and if persisted in, the ruin of many people. Some people are startled at the enormous sum of our national debt; they who understand spiritual arithmetic may well be startled if they sit down and

---

[38] From: *Forty-one Letters on Religious Subjects*. Originally Published Under the Signatures of Omicron and Vigil. Letter XXII. On the Advantages of a State of Poverty. See: *Works*, 1828, pp.85-8.
[39] *Works*, 1828, p. 87.

compute the debt of national sin'.[40] What Newton meant by 'national sin' is clear from the context; he meant infidelity, contempt of the gospel, profligacy in manners, perjury and, interestingly, 'the cry of blood, the blood of thousands, perhaps millions, from the East Indies'. He goes on, 'there is one political maxim which comforts me, "The Lord Reigns" '.[41] The sovereign rule of God, however, did not deter Newton from bending every effort to alleviate suffering wherever it was to be found within his purview. If Scripture was to govern his spiritual development, simplicity and sincerity were to be his chosen lifestyle. In his 'Omicron' correspondence[42], Letter 23 is devoted to the concept of simplicity. For Newton simplicity of both intention and dependence meant that, 'We have but one leading aim ... so that everything else in which we are concerned may be subordinate ... in a word that we are devoted to the Lord'. This 'devotion to the Lord' is because, 'He willingly endured the cross ... and laid down His life'.[43] Newton's life of simplicity and self-sacrifice in helping others finds its model in Christ. It was single minded simplicity which allowed Newton himself to be content with few worldly possessions. He had 'grown out of the desire to make money and was even free from the normal seeking after financial security'.[44]

His identification with his people took him into the homes of poor and rich alike, though the poor perhaps welcomed him more warmly than the rich. Martin's view is that 'Newton went too far in seeking familiarity with the poor'.[45] Newton went in and out of cottages because he regarded this association with the poor not only as a duty but as a delight, a delight shared by those who he visited. He was the epitome of Crabbe's parson:

---

[40] From: *Cardiphonia; or, The Utterance of the Heart in the Course of a Real Correspondence* [pp. 125-309]. Letters to Mrs P---, Letter III, August --, 1775; first published 1780. See: *Works*, 1828, p. 250.

[41] From *Cardiphonia*. See: *Works*, 1828, p. 250.

[42] A series of letters first published by Newton in 1774 under the pseudonym 'Omicron.'

[43] Letter XXIII 'On Simplicity and Godly Sincerity' [first pub. 1774], from *Forty-one Letters on Religious Subjects originally published under the signatures of Omicron and Vigil*. See: *Works*, 1828, p. 88.

[44] Martin, *Newton*, 1950, p. 218.

[45] Martin, *Newton*, 1950, p. 216.

Our Priest was cheerful, and in season gay;
His frequent visits seldom fail'd to please;
Easy himself, he sought his Neighbour's ease,...
Simple he was and lov'd the simple Truth.[46]

When Newton raised money for distribution to the poor and to purchase essential provisions it came from his wealthy London friends. Both Cowper and Newton deplored the plight of the lace makers in Olney. Cowper wrote to Parliament, 'I am an eyewitness to this poverty. There are nearly two thousand two hundred in this beggarly town, the most of whom had reason ... to look upon every loaf they bought as their last ....'[47] Newton's modus operandi was to take frequent collections for distribution to the poor. John Thornton, a rich merchant 'of the kind rarely met outside fairy tales' worked hard, spent little on himself and gave much away.[48] Newton received regularly from Thornton handsome presents of money 'for the poor folk of Olney'. His advice to Newton was, 'keep an open house ... help the poor and needy'. Thus Newton's task was the distribution to the Olney lace makers from the wealth of London's affluent commerce. During the period of Newton's curacy at Olney he received more than £3,000 for this redistribution.

Another part of Newton's social concern involved what was then described as 'idiocy' or 'lunacy'. He was particularly sensitive to such malady because it affected in various degrees his friend Cowper. Newton had been accused of driving people mad by his preaching; a possible reference to his vivid portraits of judgment and hell. Yet his own view was that the sedentary life of the women, poring over intricate lacemaking for twelve hours a day, and breathing confined air in their crowded and tiny Olney rooms, was more likely to be the cause of lunacy than his preaching. In any event, he estimates that he had more than a dozen such cases 'disordered in their heads.'

---

[46] From: *The Borough: a poem in twenty-four letters*, Letter III, 'The Vicar', by George Crabbe, first published 1810.

[47] Cited by Bernard Martin in *John Newton*, 1950, p. 234.

[48] John Thornton (1720-1790), converted under George Whitefield's preaching, was a devout evangelical Anglican philanthropist, who supported Newton with £200 a year during his curacy at Olney, further increasing his support in 1780 by offering him the living as vicar of St Mary Woolnoth.

It was a keen sense of his own shortcomings that gave Newton sympathy for any distressed person including those who had brought the trouble upon themselves. On his occasional preaching tours away from Olney, he also took opportunities to visit prisons. Frequently what he saw on such visits horrified the now sensitive Newton and he took this up with John Howard who at that time was beginning his study of English prisons.[49] Howard and Newton corresponded regularly in mutual support for the review and revision of the appalling conditions in English prisons. Newton saw it all through the eyes of a previous slave trader where he been actively involved in conditions even worse than he observed on one visit in 1770 and saw 'ye prisoners in the Gaol'.[50]

The children of Olney received much of Newton's affection. He had no children of his own and perhaps this gave him a special endearment for children in the parish, though some of them were more than a little troublesome. One Olney resident wrote of the children '... who infest the streets every evening with curses and with songs to which it would be unseemly to give their proper epithet'. Some were even later described as 'fearful groups of child savages' and linked with the 'Negro' slave trade as 'the blackest of all stains on this age'.[51] Soon after going to Olney, Newton set out to win the children's interest by telling them tales of his sailing days and helping them to make model ships. He began a weekly children's meeting, and at one stage had twenty children regularly meeting on Sundays under his tutelage and influence. Thus Newton established Sunday Schools fifteen or more years before Robert Raikes, who is generally considered as the first promoter of Sunday schools with his work starting in the 1780s.

Devotion to alleviating suffering, espousing the causes of the poor and caring for the needy made Newton a marked man in ecclesiastical circles. Not for him the life of ease and leisure characteristic of the country parson in the 18th century. It was not that the curate of Olney had no interest in or time for the country, for quietness, for seclusion

---

[49] When in 1777 John Howard published the first edition of his research, *The State of the Prisons in England and Wales, with Preliminary Observations,* he gave Newton a copy in appreciation for his help and encouragement.

[50] Martin, *Newton,* 1950, p. 214.

[51] These remarks are cited by Martin in *Newton,* 1950, 217.

and simple pleasures - but his view was ever on a higher calling, to serve God. After his induction at St Mary Woolnoth on 8 December 1779, that service was to be further exercised for twenty-eight more years in the city of London.

(ii) London (1779 -1807)

In Lombard Street at the heart of the City stood a fine example of ecclesiastical architecture by Hawksmoor, St Mary Woolnoth, which towered over the commercial centre of 18th century London. Newton's wealthy friend, John Thornton, had acquired the presentation and offered the living to Newton in the autumn of 1779, writing: 'I know of no one who will so well fill [the vacancy] as the curate of Olney'.[52] In a letter days later to another friend, Newton writes, 'My race at Olney is nearly finished. I am about to form a connection with one Mary Woolnoth, a reputed saint in Lombard Street'.[53] Newton also humorously commented, '...to wed Molly Woolnoth would be pleasing, but to be divorced from Olney would be painful'.[54] Newton wrote of his new London appointment in characteristic fashion: 'That one of the most ignorant, the most miserable, and the most abandoned of slaves, should be plucked from his forlorn state of exile on the coast of Africa, and at length be appointed minister of the parish of the first magistrate of the first city in the world - that he should there not only testify of such grace, but stand up as a singular instance and monument of it . . . is a fact I can contemplate with admiration, but never sufficiently estimate'.[55]

London life at the end of the 18th century was a marked contrast to life in Olney - yet there were the similarities of poverty and violence, and Newton was to meet both. Despite his early attempt to disguise his identity in some of his widely read publications (with noms de plume such as 'Omicron' and 'Cardiphonia'), Newton's fame as the author of these, and particularly of his autobiographical *An Authentic Narrative*, brought many influential people to St Mary Woolnoth. It also brought a

---

[52] The letter is dated 18 September 1779, and cited by Josiah Bull in *John Newton*, London, 1868, p. 238.

[53] The letter is addressed to 'Mr [William] Bull', and dated 21 September 1779; see: Josiah Bull, *John Newton*, 1868, p. 238.

[54] Newton's letter is cited by Martin in *Newton*, 1950, 271-2.

[55] From: *Memoirs of the Rev. John Newton* by R. Cecil [first published 1808]. See: *Works*, 1828, p. 53.

lifestyle quite different to that at Olney. In a letter to his old friend William Cowper, he wrote, 'Indeed I live a strange life. It looks ... only a busy idleness. My time is divided between running about to look on other people, and sitting at home like a tame Elephant or a Monkey for other people to come and look at me'.[56] The Newton's new residence[57] was some distance from the parish church and became the meeting place for ministers, friends and others who sought the counsel of the new vicar.

Conversation at his popular breakfast parties soon began to turn to the iniquity of the slave trade. He would say, 'My heart shudders that I was ever engaged in it'.[58] As early as 1774, John Wesley had written a powerful pamphlet on the evils of the slave trade[59], and an aversion to such iniquity was at last coming to the public conscience. On the other hand, it could hardly be abolished without harm to the national economy. Only an Act of Parliament could bring abolition, but even in 1785 Newton could see no cause for optimism. In December of that year a decisive event occurred when William Wilberforce, an able and influential Member of Parliament, requested an interview with Newton. Wilberforce had already been influenced by the Methodists though not attached to them. A greater influence on Wilberforce was Isaac Milner[60], an evangelist and Yorkshire man who persuaded him to read Doddridge's *Rise and Progress of Religion in the Soul*[61], which brought Wilberforce to evangelical religion and conversion in 1787. Newton was able to further establish Wilberforce in his new faith and also to encourage him in the anti-slavery campaign.

---

[56] Cited by Martin in *Newton*, 1950, p. 276.

[57] The St Mary Woolnoth vicarage had been rented out to the post office, and so Newton rented a sizeable three-storey house with a garden about a mile away at 13 Charles Square.

[58] Cited by John Pollock, *Amazing Grace*, 1981, p. 173.

[59] John Wesley, *Thoughts Upon Slavery*, Printed by R. Hawes, London, 1774; a facsimile of this publication is reproduced in: Warren Thomas Smith, *John Wesley and Slavery*, Nashville, 1986, pp. 121-148.

[60] Isaac Milner (1750-1820), born in Leeds, became Professor of Mathematics at Cambridge, and famously encouraged Wilberforce before the 1789 Parliamentary debate, saying: 'If you carry this point, in your whole life, that life will be better spent than in being prime minister of many years.'

[61] Independent minister Philip Doddridge (1702–1751), had been a friend of John Wesley, and one of his most influential books was *The Rise and Progress of Religion in the Soul, illustrated in a course of serious and practical addresses. ... With a devout meditation, or prayer, added to each chapter*, London, 1745.

The story of anti- slavery belongs, perhaps, more to Wilberforce than to Newton. Yet it should not be overlooked that Newton, from his unique position as an ex-slave trader exercised a profound influence on Wilberforce and the inner circle of abolitionists, far beyond his expectations if not his hopes. His connection with Hannah More, playwright and society lady was almost equally influential. Newton drew Hannah More into an evangelical faith and taught her 'how to place her faith in Christ and her pen at Christ's disposal'.[62] And, she too, was to play her part in the struggle against slave-trading.

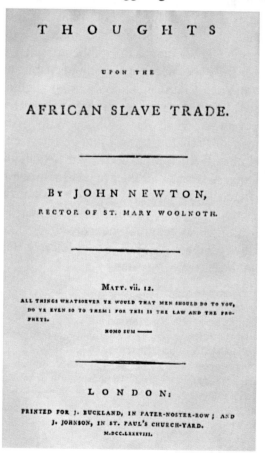

Fig 6. Title page of Newton's powerful 1788 abolitionist pamphlet

[62] Cited by Pollock, *Amazing Grace*, 1981, p. 176.

At the height of the abolition battle, Newton put pen to paper in a pamphlet which had a profound effect on the campaign. He was the only abolitionist leader with *first-hand* experience of the evil which they sought to eradicate from the national life and conscience. 'Silence, at such a time and on such an occasion, would, in me, be criminal .... I am bound in conscience to take shame to myself by a public confession, which, however sincere, comes too late to prevent or repair the misery and mischief to which I have, formerly, been accessory.'[63]

In 1788, when the venerable Newton had reached his sixty-third year, came perhaps the crowning glory of his social work. The Prime Minister, William Pitt, called the Privy Council to investigate all the aspects of the slave trade and its abolition prior to an Act of Parliament. The efforts of Wilberforce, Newton, Hannah More, and others were coming to a successful conclusion. Newton was called as a witness in the enquiry. As he entered the room, the Prime Minister and Privy Councillors rose to their feet as a mark of respect for the ex-slave trader and now Vicar of St Mary Woolnoth. But such was Newton's spirituality that he re-directed any fame and glory away from himself, 'O Lord, it is all Thy doing, to Thee be also the praise. To me belongs the shame and confusion of face, for I am a poor vile creature to this hour'.[64]

Newton, in all his writings, sermons, campaigns and concerns had taken to heart the words of Christ who had so remarkably transformed his life; '... Whosoever would be great among you must be your servant and whoever would be first among you must be slave of all' (Mark 10:43-44).

---

[63] John Newton, *Thoughts upon the African Slave Trade*, London, 1788, p. 2. A copy of this well-argued pamphlet was freely sent to every MP; it sold so well that reprinting was required immediately. See Fig. 6.

[64] Cited by Pollock, *Amazing Grace*, 1981, p. 177.

POSTSCRIPT

It may seem almost irrelevant to present the experiences and work of John Newton, an eighteenth-century man, as a role-model for the twenty-first century. But the author is persuaded that this would be a superficial view.

Evangelical spirituality has its origins in the person and saving work of Christ, the experiences of the first-century church and the extant writings of the apostles. John Newton came to embrace the essential and eternal truths of the Gospel as he faced them in his time - and those truths have not changed in their essential nature. The nature of Scripture is unchanging despite the proliferation of modern 'versions'. Today's church may tamper with the presentation of the gospel but its essential nature remains unchanged and unchangeable.

The nature of unbelieving mankind in the present century remains as it was in the first-century of the Christian era, and as it was in Newton's century; and the mountainous ego dominates mankind now as it always has. The consequences of a sinful nature express themselves in our times as they have in times past. Only the powerful, life-changing message of the gospel of Jesus Christ can effect the radical change required.

> 'For I am not ashamed of the Gospel of Christ it is the power of God to salvation for everyone who believes ...'   Romans 1:16 (NKJV)
> 'Let your light so shine before men that they may see your good works and glorify your Father in heaven'.   Matthew 5:16 (NKJV)

Newton in his day would have endorsed the words of Jesus, and His apostle Paul. So must we in our time.

SELECT BIBLIOGRAPHY[65]

Aitken, Jonathan. *John Newton: From Disgrace to Amazing Grace.* London: Continuum UK, 2007.

Backhouse, Halcyon (ed.). *Collected Letters; John Newton: Cardiphonia, or The Utterance of the Heart in the Course of a Real Correspondence.* London: Hodder & Stoughton, 1989.

Bebbington, D.W. *Evangelicalism in Modern Britain: A History from the 1730s to the 1980s.* London: Routledge, 1993.

Bull, Josiah. *John Newton of Olney and St. Mary Woolnoth: An Autobiography and Narrative, Compiled Chiefly from his Diary and Other Unpublished Documents.* Second Edition. London: The Religious Tract Society, 1868.

Cecil, R. (ed.). *The Works of The Rev. John Newton, Late Rector of the United Parishes of St. Mary Woolnoth and St. Mary Woolchurch-Haw, Lombard Street, London. Containing an Authentic Narrative, &c., Letters on Religious Subjects, Cardiphonia, Discourses intended for the Pulpit, Sermons Preached in the Parish Church of Olney, A Review of Ecclesiastical History, Olney Hymns, Poems, Messiah, Occasional Sermons, and Tracts. To which are prefixed Memoirs of his Life, &c.* Complete in one volume. Edinburgh: Peter Brown and Thomas Nelson, 1828.

Edwards, Brian. *Through Many Dangers: The Story of John Newton.* Welwyn: Evangelical Press, 1985.

Gordon, James M. *Evangelical Spirituality: [From the Wesleys to John Stott].* London: SPCK, 1991.

Hindmarsh, D. Bruce. *John Newton and the Evangelical Tradition: Between the Conversions of Wesley and Wilberforce.* Grand Rapids, Michigan/Cambridge, UK: William B. Eerdmans Publishing Company, 1996.

Martin, Bernard. *John Newton: A Biography.* London: William

---

[65] Note: several items, some published since this essay was first prepared in 1996, have been added to the original bibliography for this Wesley Fellowship publication, such as the two biographies of Newton by D.B. Hindmarsh and J. Aitken, which each have extensive and scholarly bibliographies of their own which would be helpful to a reader wishing to learn more of Newton's life and ministry.

Heinemann Ltd, 1950.

Martin, Bernard. *An Ancient Mariner: A Biography of John Newton.* London: Wyvern Books, 1960.

Newton, John. *Thoughts upon the African Slave Trade*, London, 1788. [A copy of this publication was accessible on 15 September 2011 at <http://www.archive.org/details/thoughtsuponafri00newt>]

[Newton, John]. *Letters of John Newton.* Letters 1-7 and 10-19 are from letters signed *Omicron* (1774) and *Vigil* (1785); the remainder are from Newton's best-known work, *Cardiphonia* (1781). Edinburgh: The Banner of Truth Trust, 1960, reprinted 1984.

[Newton, John]. *John Newton. Out of the Depths: An Autobiography.* [The Letters were written to the Rev. T. Haweis, D.D., and were first published in 1764]. Chicago: Moody Press, n.d.

[Newton, John and William Cowper]. *Olney Hymns in Three Books: Facsimile of the First Edition* [1779]. Olney: The Trustees of the Cowper and Newton Museum, 1979.

Peterson, W.I. and W.A. Hutchinson (eds*.).* *Out of the Depths.* Lincolnwood, Illinois: Keats Publishing Ltd, 1981.

Pollock, John. *Amazing Grace: John Newton's Story.* London: Hodder and Stoughton, 1981.

Smith, Warren Thomas. *John Wesley and Slavery.* Nashville: Abingdon Press, 1986.

Styles, Jim. *Let's Talk About Olney's Amazing Curate.* Privately Published, c.1983. [Proceeds to Olney Parish Church Heating Fund].

[Wesley, John]. *The Works of John Wesley.* [Bicentennial Edition, Vols 1-33 projected]. Vol. 1, Sermons I, ed. Albert C. Outler, Nashville: Abingdon Press, 1984.

Fig 7. An artist's impression of John Newton's London church, St. Mary's Woolnoth, as it looked in 2010